Successful
Decision-Making

in a week

Malcolm Peel

eadway · Hodder & Stoughton

Acknowledgement

The practical approach of Charles Kepner and Ben Tregoe
(*The New Rational Manager*, 1981, John Martin) has been
particularly helpful to me in thinking about many aspects of
this subject.

British Library Cataloguing in Publication Data
A catalogue record for this title is available from the British Library

ISBN 0 340 63154 6

First published 1995
Impression number 10 9 8 7 6 5 4 3 2 1
Year   1999 1998 1997 1996 1995

Typeset by Multiplex Techniques Ltd, Orpington, Kent.
Printed in Great Britain for Hodder & Stoughton Educational,
a division of Hodder Headline Plc, 338 Euston Road, London
NW1 3BH by St Edmundsbury Press, Bury St Edmunds
Suffolk.

**the Institute
of Management**

F O U N D A T I O N

The Institute of Management (IM) is at the forefront of
management development and best management
practice. The Institute embraces all levels of
management from students to chief executives. It
provides a unique portfolio of services for all
managers, enabling them to develop skills and achieve
management excellence.

For information on the benefits of membership, please
write to:

Department HS
Institute of Management
Cottingham Road
Corby
Northants NN17 1TT
Tel. 01536 204222
Fax 01536 201651

This series is commissioned by the Institute of
Management Foundation.

C O N T E N T S

Decisions, decisions... It is impossible to escape them. What shoes should I wear today? Which is the best route to the airport? Which candidate should we select for the vacancy? How should I invest my money? What price should we set for our new product? Which software package should we buy for our new pcs?

The consequences of making a wrong decision can vary from a slight annoyance to a major catastrophe. Sometimes it is possible to change our mind; often it is not.

Serious decision-making involves many aspects of our personality; courage, intelligence, experience, training, beliefs and preconceptions. For some, it is a matter of instinct; for some, of painstaking analysis. Some of us thrive on risky decisions; some prefer to reduce risk to a minimum.

This book aims to be of practical value to all; especially to those in management, for a manager must be an effective decision-maker. It touches on the main aspects of decision-making, emphasising that effective decisions need a genuinely open mind, sound common sense, and courage, and covers:

Sunday	The process
Monday	Definition
Tuesday	Criteria
Wednesday	Options
Thursday	Decision-making aids
Friday	Group decision-making
Saturday	Decision review

The process

Today, we will look at the basics of decision-making:

- What is a decision?
- Other modes of thought
- The decision-making process

What is a decision?

It is surprisingly difficult to define a decision. The word is used in many different ways and can, if we are not careful, cover almost any type of thinking process. To keep the situation manageable and be of maximum practical value, we shall concentrate this week on one area of meaning.

A **decision** is: *The formation of an intention to behave in a certain way.*

Decisions are in the mind. An 'intention' is a mental act; it is often described as 'making up our mind'. Logic, therefore, should be important, but decisions must also involve commitment; at the end of the day they can only be made by people, not machines. Decisions must also look to the future; to an intended course of behaviour.

Other modes of thought

We do not spend our whole life making decisions (thank goodness!). One of the commonest causes of confusion and difficulty is failing, as it were, to get our thinking into the right gear. During the course of any 24 hours, we use our mind in many different ways. We may be in passive, receptive mode; watching TV, eating, relaxing in the sun or in front of the fire. We may be preoccupied with our feelings; angry, loving, distressed, or frustrated. Or we may be actively switched on to some demanding mental task.

Decisions may be made in any of these modes. If we are passive and relaxed, we may decide to put our feet up and have a snooze, eat another packet of crisps or pour ourselves a drink. If we are in the grip of feelings, we may walk out of the room, break off a relationship, or make a proposal of marriage. However, this week it is the rational mode of thought that concerns us. This does not mean that our decision-making must necessarily be devoid of feeling, but the feelings must not be allowed to override the logic.

Even within active, rational thinking, there are many different ways our mind may work, depending on the task in front of us. To be effective, we must employ the mode of thought which is most appropriate to our situation; only failure can result from trying to make a decision when, for example, we should be solving a problem. It is helpful to consider some of the modes of rational thought that are related to, but different from, decision-making . These include:

- Judging
- Problem-solving
- Planning
- Routine

Judging
The word 'decide' can be used to mean to settle or resolve a question, in the way that a court of law tries and decides a case. But judgements look backwards, weighing up events that have already taken place or situations that already exist. They also do not necessarily commit the person judging to a course of action.

Problem-solving
Some writers use the words 'problem' and 'decision' interchangeably; others even speak of a 'decision problem'.

Kepner-Tregoe (*The New Rational Manager*, 1981), on the other hand, make a clear and useful distinction between a problem and a decision, pointing out that each needs its own, very different method of thought.

They define a problem as a situation in which we are seeking the cause of something that has gone wrong – a 'deviation from a standard'. As an example, let us suppose that, in trying to start our car, when we turn the ignition key the engine does not burst into life. This is certainly a deviation from a standard; the engine should fire. Whether it presents us with a 'problem' or a 'decision' will depend on the exact situation.

On the one hand, we may not know why the engine has not started. It may be a loose wire, damp, dirt, a faulty coil, a broken fuel pump, or something else. In this case, we must problem-solve – i.e. establish the cause – before we can decide what action to take. If we do not, there is a serious danger of wasting effort and time. It will not help us to charge the battery, for example, if the starter has jammed or the wiring come loose.

On the other hand, we may know the cause; we may realise that the battery is flat. In this case, we do not have a 'problem', but a decision; our need is to decide what to do about it. Should we, for example, put it on charge, use jump leads to connect to another battery, or summon the AA?

If we have experienced a problem, decision-making will follow naturally. Once we have identified the cause of our engine's failure to start, we must move on to deciding what to do about it. However, in many cases there will not have been a problem we needed to solve; we will be faced straight away with the need for a decision.

Planning
Planning is the process of working out **how** something will be done, rather than making the decision of **what** should be done.

We may decide, for example, to rent and open one of four available retail shops. Before we can do so, however, we will need to make a plan covering all aspects of the opening; obtaining a bank loan, briefing a solicitor, arranging when and how we will furnish it, stock it up, staff it, promote it, and open its doors.

Planning often requires further decision-making on a series of smaller points (a 'decision chain'). Occasionally, if some important new aspect is thrown up, it may even cause us to go back to the original decision. Until we started planning, for example, we may not have discovered that a similar shop was to be opened two streets away.

Planning can be a complex process, and has its own range of specialised techniques. This also is outside the scope of our thinking this week.

Routine
Conscious thought is hardly needed for many of the actions we take every day in our domestic, working and leisure lives. We can rarely be said to make a decision to travel to work by our usual route, or handle our routine correspondence according to our normal methods, unless there is something unusual about the circumstances

(flooding or strike, a new secretary etc.) the mental processes involved are virtually automatic.

The proportion of our work we handle in this way, without the need for conscious decision, will vary according to our role; managers and creative artists, for example, are likely to need to take more frequent decisions than workers on a production line.

What is routine for one person may require much thought by another. A skilled craftsman may for example, plaster a ceiling without the need for a single conscious decision. A DIY amateur faced with the same task may need much conscious decision-making, planning – even problem-solving – before success is attained.

The decision-making process

In the introduction, we suggested that three ingredients were essential for effective decisions: a genuinely open mind, sound common sense, and courage. Decisions of any

importance or complexity also need the support of a
framework or process within which to exercise these
qualities to best effect. Here is such a process:

1 Defining the decision
2 Setting the criteria
3 Finding options
4 Choosing decision-making aids
5 Deciding
6 Reviewing

Is our mind open?
Unless we begin with a genuinely open mind, there is no
point in following a process. It has been said that 'Minds
appear not to need making up; it is un-making them which
takes time and evidence' (R J Audley in *Decision-Making*,
1967, BBC). Indeed, the common approach in many
situations is: 'I believe A is the thing to do. Let me find
evidence to support A'.

We may feel as soon as they walk into our office that a
certain candidate is perfect for the post we are filling. We
may have fallen in love with the weekend cottage we saw
on holiday. We may be determined that our next car must
be a Ferrari. From this point, the mind subconsciously
selects evidence to support our chosen decision, whilst
ignoring, or misinterpreting, evidence that points the other
way. In these situations, a rational decision-making process
would be a sham and a waste of time.

There need be nothing wrong with irrational or instinctive
decisions; some of the most crucial decisions in both

personal and working lives are taken in this way. A rational decision-making process is appropriate when **a)** we are in doubt and **b)** we are sufficiently open-minded to follow where it leads.

We will now look briefly at each step in the process.

1   Defining the decision

Defining our decision is the essential starting point for any rational process. Until we have cleared our mind as to exactly **what** we are deciding, why, and who is involved in making the decision, any further thought runs the risk of confusion and error.

As an example, we can suppose that we are one of four members of a family in a car at a crossroads, deciding which road to take. Our **aim** may be to get to back home in time for tea.

We will examine this step tomorrow.

2   Setting the criteria

Every decision requires one or more **criteria** by which the available options will be judged. Thus, in the example, our travellers may be concerned to avoid heavily crowded roads, to use a scenic route, and to minimise the cost of the journey.

We will look at this step on Tuesday.

3   Finding options

If we know that there is only one course open to us, then we have no decision to make. Normally, there will be a number of options, and the process must involve establishing what these are.

In our example, three choices are obvious; at the crossroads, each road offers an option. At this stage in the process, new options will often become apparent; we may add, for example, the possibility of going back the way we have come.

We will look at this step on Wednesday.

4   Choosing decision-making aids

Choosing between the options will call for the help of one or more aids. At one end of the scale, we could decide to toss a coin; at the other we could decide to undertake a rigorous and structured matching process between our objectives and the available options.

The chosen aid will need to be appropriate to the importance of the decision and the time and other resources available. Our family at the crossroads is unlikely to feel it necessary to construct a mathematical model of each route in order to assess the probability distribution of expected arrival times using each.

We will look at this step on Thursday, and consider group decision-making methods on Friday.

5   *Deciding*

The chosen methods should now be used to help make the decision. Doing so will almost always involve gathering relevant information, and frequently requires us to forecast the likely future conditions and outcomes of possible actions.

Our family will now use information from their map, perhaps supplemented by their own knowledge, enquiries made of a passer-by or perhaps traffic reports on the radio. They may also need to assess the probability of a traffic jam, perhaps even the effect of the expected weather on each route.

6   *Reviewing*

Before springing into action, it is always sensible to recheck the process and the data we have used, and also ask questions such as, 'If we now do this, what might go wrong?' to throw up any aspects or factors we may have missed.

A member of our family may, perhaps suddenly recollect that there were roadworks on one of the routes, or that it has a railway level crossing at which delays are frequent.

We will look at this step on Saturday.

Summary

- A decision is 'the formation of an intention to behave in a certain way'. It is a mental process, which cannot be mechanical
- It is essential to choose the correct mode of thinking. We must be active and logical, and distinguish decision-making from judging, problem-solving, planning and routine thought
- Rational decision-making calls for an open mind, otherwise there is no point in trying to use a logical process
- Rational decision-making has six steps: definition, setting aim and criteria, finding options, choosing aids, deciding, and reviewing

Defining the decision

Today, we will look at the first step in the decision-making process we described yesterday:

Step 1 – Definition
- Is there a decision to be made?
- How urgent is it?
- Who should make it?
- Defining the decision
- The aim

Is there a decision to be made?

Realising that there is real need for a decision is the essential starting point for the process. There are twin dangers: failing to make a necessary decision, or making a decision that is unnecessary.

Failing to take necessary decisions
In both personal and professional life, it is easy, and can
sometimes be disastrous, not to realise that a decision must
be faced. There is the temptation to soldier on with
unsatisfactory situations, out-dated products, machinery or
processes, to accept less than satisfactory performance from
individuals, or to fail to notice the signs of an oncoming
financial crisis.

One common cause of this reluctance is fear of change:
'Better the devil we know than the devil we don't.' Change
is always demanding, and can be painful, but failure to
make a necessary change can lead to disaster.

Another cause can be the difficulty of detecting slow, long-
term movements. We all live at a set speed, and events may
be either too fast or too slow for us to spot easily. Slow
changes are the hardest to detect. It is often difficult, for
example, to pick up a slow deterioration in performance,
whether of an individual or a piece of machinery.
Distinguishing between random and significant variations
in a series of data and forecasting trends presents a major
statistical challenge. Many organisations, including some of
the largest and most sophisticated, have failed to pick up
long-term changes in the market place, their competition, or
the economic climate.

Spotting the need for decisions calls for a systematic and
proactive approach; we can never sit back. Amongst the
steps that will help are:

- Set and use clear performance standards
- Regularly review all aspects of the operation
- Use suitable statistical techniques to monitor time series of important data
- Control finances and budgets
- Regularly review the performance of competitors, suppliers and customers
- Monitor the general economic and financial climate and outlook
- Be aware of developments in technologies, materials, products and services

Making unnecessary decisions

Like the gardener who was for ever taking up his plants to see if the roots were growing properly, there is a danger in disturbing situations unnecessarily.

We may be tempted to do this following a previous decision. Perhaps we have changed the way something is done, introduced new machinery or equipment, or recruited a new member of staff. In such situations, everyone naturally looks for improved results. If these do not appear as soon as we expect or would like, we may start to feel that the change was a mistake, and wonder whether we should change back (if this is possible) or make further changes.

Occasionally, there is the temptation to change for change's sake. We may feel bored or stale. We may feel the need to convince people that we are being positive and proactive. Others may be pressurising us to act. We may even want to divert attention from something else that is not as it should be.

Here are some suggestions for avoiding unnecessary decisions:

- Set and use clear performance standards
- Give previous decisions sufficient time to show results
- Resist pressure from sales techniques, fashion etc.
- Never believe that frequent decision-making indicates a strong character

How urgent is the decision?

As much harm can be done by rushing a decision for which we have plenty of time, as by taking our time over a decision that is needed immediately.

Urgency and importance are not the same. **Importance** is the measure of a decision's overall effect; **urgency** is the time available to make it. A decision about the launching of a new product range is likely to be very important; it would affect the whole future of the organisation, but it will probably not be urgent. On the other hand, a decision about whether to let our assistant take leave tomorrow will be very urgent, but is unlikely to be important. To distinguish the two will help us to put a decision in perspective.

Sources of time pressure
We should probe the real nature of any time pressures that we feel. Quite often, there may be more flexibility than at first appears. Pressure may originate from inside ourselves, from other people, or from circumstances.

A feeling of urgency often comes from inside. The need to make even a simple decision causes a degree of stress for most people. We may feel the urge to escape from the stress by making a quick choice. Some people believe, wrongly, that delay in decision-making shows weakness, and haste shows strength of character. This conviction has even become part of the language; the word 'decisive' conveys overtones of speed, and 'hesitant' and 'indecisive' are virtual synonyms. A moment's reflection convinces most people that this is not true.

Pressure to decide quickly may come from other people. They too may be seeking, perhaps subconsciously, to relieve the stress they feel. Sometimes the pressure may be part of a deliberate stratagem to force a decision that is favourable to them. We have all met the salesman's or buyer's ploy, 'The company is putting the price up by 10% next week; I told them I had promised you, but I can only hold it until tonight. . .', 'Chap has just phoned me up asking if I had one of these. I told him I'd get back to him straight away, but that you must have first refusal. . .', 'The first three buyers will have a chance to win a holiday for two in Miami. . .'.

Time pressure from circumstances, on the other hand, must always be taken seriously. If the ship is sinking or the office on fire, we will not want to do too much detailed analysis. But even then, we will need to remind ourselves that the greater the crisis, the greater the need for the best decision we can make. Decision-makers who rush around like scalded cats are a danger to themselves and others; a correct decision made in 30 seconds is better than a wrong one made in five. The more familiar we are with the step-by-step process described in this book, the better we shall be able to focus on the essential and reject the unimportant.

Interim decisions
Some form of holding action designed to relieve time pressure – to buy time – may occasionally be justified. We may need to gather more information or more friends. We may hope circumstances will change in our favour, or a

problem solve itself. A sensible interim decision can be better than a premature final decision.

Who should take the decision?

Three groups of people are involved in decisions; those who:

- Take them
- Must carry them out
- Will be affected by them

Even the most personal decision – to resign from our post, for example – will usually affect others apart from ourselves: colleagues, family, perhaps clients. Occasionally, all three groups (or individuals) may be the same. In most cases, however, the three groups are distinct. A decision to close a branch outlet, for example, may be made by the Board, carried out by branch management, and affect both staff and customers. It is essential to define each group, and consider what their involvement should be on the way a decision is made.

Those making the decision
The first question to be answered is: Who has the authority to make this decision?

This may be clear and defined; it may be our personal choice, and ours alone. In an organisation, there may be instructions, for example, that all purchases of capital equipment costing more than £1 000 require the approval of a director. In other cases, authority may not be so clear. We may have to clarify our position, for example, before speaking to the media about company policy, or sacking an employee.

We should also ask: Who can contribute to this decision?

It is foolish to insist on making a decision ourselves if we can call on the help of those with greater experience and expertise.

We may also need to ask: Who will expect to be involved?

There are frequently those who expect to be a party to a decision, and who may be able to frustrate decisions taken without their involvement.

Occasionally, we would be wise to ask: Who (if anyone) should **not** be involved?

There may be a reason for excluding some whose involvement might be more damaging than their omission.

Those carrying out the decision
More and more managers believe that decision-making should be participative and involve those who must carry out a decision. Some managers now go even further, regarding their role as 'empowering' their people; that is, encouraging and helping them to make their own decisions in the widest possible range of situations.

Managers who adopt these styles must be effective communicators. They must also be secure enough to accept the reality of others' power in decision-making, and the possibility of decisions being made that they may not agree with.

Those affected

Involving those who may be affected by a decision can raise difficult issues. Unpopular decisions might be virtually impossible to make in this way. It is unlikely, for example, that a decision to raise prices, close down an operation, or sack large numbers of employees could be made if all those who may be affected were involved.

In some cases, the numbers of those affected may be very large: the customers of a large retail chain, for example, the shareholders of a large limited company, or the ratepayers of a county. In government and formal organisations this difficulty is overcome by the election of representatives of those involved: councillors, members of parliament etc. In management decision-making, trade unions, works councils and staff associations may perform the same role. In less formal situations, we may need to carry out surveys or conduct market research on representative samples of those who would be affected.

We will return to group decision-making on Friday.

Defining the decision

The more accurately we define the decision to be taken, the better will be its chances of success. Unless we clarify our thinking right at the start we risk wasting time and other resources, backtracking, confusing ourselves and others, and finally making inappropriate or ineffective decisions.

Effective decision definitions should be:

- Written
- Correctly positioned in the chain
- Clear, simple and accurate
- Not option-based

Written
If we have time, it is always helpful to commit the decision definition to paper. A written decision definition helps clear and precise thinking, strengthens our commitment, makes communication easier and more effective, and provides a record for future reference.

Correctly positioned in the chain
Decisions may be thought of as linked together in chains. The act of trying to write a definition frequently shows us that we are not at the point on the chain we thought we had reached. Thus if we write our decision definition as: 'Choosing which of the office premises available in Malvern to rent', this implies that we have already decided that:

1 We need new (or additional) office premises
2 We are only considering premises in Malvern
3 We will only consider renting

4 We must choose from what is now available; we cannot wait for further, possibly more suitable, premises to come on the market

If we realise that the need has not been analysed (**1**), the decision definition could be rewritten: 'Deciding whether additional office accommodation is necessary'.

If we realise the need has been established, but the location has not been considered (**2**), our decision definition could be: 'Choosing which areas to search for additional office accommodation'.

Alternatively, we might take a different approach at this point in the chain, and include location, the rent/buy aspect and timescale as three of the criteria to be taken into account in making our decision. If we tackle our decision in this way, we could rewrite the decision definition: 'Choosing additional office accommodation'.

If we have decided we are only interested in Malvern, but both the rent/buy and time scale are still open (**3** and **4**), the decision definition might be: 'Choosing office premises in Malvern to rent or buy'.

Clear, simple and accurate
Effective decision definitions must, like other aspects of the decision-making process, be as accurate as we can make them. Sloppy or ambiguous words risk the possibility of sloppy and ineffective decisions.

We might, for example, write: 'To decide whether we need new offices, how much space they should have, where they should be, whether we need parking and whether we should rent or buy.'

This definition is too loose and complicated to be helpful. The latter part presupposes the result of the first part (i.e. that we **do** need new offices). It implies that the decision now being taken is **which** new office to choose, but does not say so. It lists some of the criteria by which this second decision could be taken (amount of space, location, car parking and rent/buy). There will be others which are not listed. None need to be specified in the definition; they will be considered later.

Depending on what the situation is, we might rewrite the definition as: 'Choosing additional office premises'.

The criteria listed in the original definition would be used, almost certainly along with others, in making the choice. We will discuss the use of criteria tomorrow.

Not option-based
In practice, most people first feel the need to make a decision when confronted with a choice. As in our example of yesterday, we may find ourselves, metaphorically or in reality, at a crossroads, uncertain which road to take. It may be through an advertisement: 'Look! They've brought out a new GTIX1000'; a chance conversation: 'I've just met

someone who tells me that we could sell our machinery and lease it back'; a paragraph in the papers: 'This Investors in People thing seems very popular, should we go in for it?'; or perhaps our own thought sequences: 'If I buy a modem, I might be able to work from home'. There is, of course, nothing intrinsically wrong with this method of thinking, but it can lead to difficulties. If we wait until we are prompted by the appearance of a choice, we may define the decision too narrowly.

Here are some typical option-based decisions:

1 Deciding whether or not to upgrade our word-processing package to the latest version
2 Choosing which PR consultancy to employ
3 Whether to put the new draughtsman in Pete's office or Mary's
4 Deciding where to hold the Christmas party this year

In each of the cases above, we have defined the decision in terms of the options, either explicitly (**1** and **3**), or that we are confident exist (**2** and **4**). By doing so, we run the risk of missing other options which might be more suitable and possibly ending with a course of action which does not meet our real needs. After a little thought, we might find a different and sounder starting point.

Decision **1** may be called a **binary** decision; whether to do something or not. Many decisions first present themselves in this form, but it is always best to ensure that such decisions are **a**) necessary (maybe we started thinking only because we read an advertisement in the paper, but our present word-processing package is doing all we need), and **b**) correctly defined (perhaps we could improve our word-processing capability in other ways).

We may feel that decision **2** is correctly stated; we have already agreed on the need to employ a PR consultancy, and must now choose one.

Decision **3** may, on reflection, be expressed too narrowly; there may be other office places vacant and rearrangements possible. We will rephrase it without alternatives: 'Where to locate the new draughtsman'.

Decision **4** may raise the question of whether we really want a Christmas party. Some people may want nothing; others a lunch or dinner; others a cash bonus. We may end up by rephrasing this: 'Whether and how to celebrate Christmas as an organisation'.

The aim

Just as, however great the time pressure, we should always define the decision we are making, so we should always clarify the aim.

'Decision definition' and 'aim'
The decision definition and aim are not the same. The **definition** describes the decision we are taking. The **aim**

describes **why** we are making it; the overall result we wish to achieve. Thus if our decision definition is: 'Selecting a car-hire organisation to provide our company fleet for the next three years', the aim of the decision might be: 'To provide the fleet of company cars in the most efficient and cost-effective way'.

If our decision definition is: 'Choosing the menu for the annual dinner', the aim of the decision is likely to be: 'To provide a meal that staff enjoy at a cost we can afford'.

The aim will normally begin 'In order to . . .' or simply, 'To. . .'.

Sometimes, an accurate definition and clear aim will be the key to the whole process, and lead us straight to the correct decision.

Summary

- We must be sure that a decision is needed
- 'Urgency' and 'importance' are not the same. We must assess the urgency of a decision coolly and resist unjustifiable pressure
- Making an interim decision may sometimes help
- We should consider those who must make a decision, those who must carry it out, and those whom it will affect
- The decision must be defined and its aim clarified before going further
- It is usually better for decisions not to be option based

Setting the criteria

Just as, however great the time pressure, we should always define the decision we are making so we should devote some time to clarifying the criteria. For an urgent, unplanned decision, we might only be able to spare a few seconds. In an important decision for which we have sufficient time, it might take days or even weeks. Either way, the phase is essential; the definition, aim and criteria form the foundation for success.

Today we will consider:

Step 2 – Criteria
- What are criteria?
- Types of criteria
- Criteria setting
- Criteria or options first?

What are the criteria?

Criteria are any other considerations that matter to us in respect of the decision, and against which we will compare the options.

Our decision definition, for example, may be: 'Choosing the mix of products we should aim to sell in the next financial year', and the aim: 'To maximise our net profits from sales'.

A few moments' thought will show that other considerations we have in making this decision could include:

a Not needing to raise additional finance
b Contributing to the overall image and market position of the business
c Not damaging the long-term goodwill of the business
d Using the skills of the existing workforce
e That we enjoy selling

These would be our criteria, and we will use them to choose between the options available.

Occasionally, the aim may be the only aspect of the decision which matters to us. If, for example, our decision definition is: 'Choosing a route to take to escape from this burning building', and the aim: 'To stay alive' other criteria, if they exist at all, will be unimportant. Decisions of this kind revolve around the finding of options, a step in the sequence which we will look at tomorrow.

Types of criteria

Criteria can be of three kinds: **resource** criteria (**a** and **d** in the example above), **feature** criteria (**e** above), and **outcome** criteria (**b** and **c** above). They may be either positive – outcomes we would like, or negative – outcomes we wish to avoid. We will now look at each type of objective.

Resource criteria define the resources that the decision-maker is able and willing to commit to the implementation of the decision. They are thus likely to be within the control of the decision-maker. They may include:

- Capital costs
- Running costs
- Time constraints
- Manpower and skill constraints
- Organisational factors
- Geographical/locational factors

Feature criteria are those which describe features we wish the decision to provide. Examples of feature criteria are:

For choice of computer software:
- Full networking capability

For choice of office accommodation
- At least 1 000 square feet of usable space

For selection of a worker:
- Time-served pattern-maker

Features are of no value in themselves, but are of value for the results we hope they will achieve. We actually want the networking capability to allow work-stations to exchange data as easily as possible; the office space in order to accommodate the staff, furniture and equipment we expect to need; and the time-serving to ensure the recruit has the pattern-making skills we require.

Despite this, feature criteria can be very helpful in decision-making, because we can check whether an available option meets them. Thus we can establish whether the software has networking capability before buying it, and whether the candidate served an apprenticeship before recruiting him or her. This cannot be done with outcome criteria.

Considering the options available will often suggest feature criteria. If, for example, we have talked with a sales representative, or looked through catalogues, we are likely to be attracted to some of the features offered by the products, whether we had previously thought of them or not. 'Oh, look' we may say, 'they offer numerically

controlled material feed. What a good idea! We must have
that.' This can be helpful; we may not have realised that
numerically controlled material feed could be provided. But
there are also dangers; it is easy to be over sold on features
we don't actually need. We should always challenge feature
criteria, and decide whether it would be more effective to
express them in terms of our real needs, as outcome criteria.

Outcome criteria are the results that the decision-maker
wishes the decision to produce. The aim will always be the
principle outcome, but there are often others. Thus, if our
decision definition is: 'Choosing the best method of travel to
Glasgow', and our aim: 'To arrive by 1530 tomorrow',
outcome criteria could include:

- Maximum safety
- A relaxed journey
- Unaffected by weather conditions

Because, unlike feature criteria, outcome criteria look to the future, all we can do is to estimate the probability that an option will meet them. We can consider the likelihood of car, rail, air and coach travel being safe, relaxed and unaffected by weather, but we cannot know for certain how any of them will actually turn out.

Criteria setting

As with the decision definition and aim, if our decision is important and the time is available, it is always a good idea to commit our objectives to paper. In doing this, the following steps will help:

1 Generate a list of possible criteria
2 Edit the criteria produced
3 Weight the criteria

1   Generate a list of possible criteria
The aim at this stage should be to write down every possibility, without attempting to edit or criticise it; we will do this in the next step. Whilst some criteria will be immediately obvious, others may need considerable thought. It can be a great help to involve other people; brainstorming often helps to spark off ideas.

If we already have options in mind, they can be a helpful starting point in generating criteria. Considering what attracts us and what we are unhappy about with each option often suggests criteria.

Let us suppose in making the decision about the journey to Glasgow we generate the following criteria:

- Maximum safety
- A relaxed journey
- Unaffected by weather conditions
- Comfortable
- Cheap
- Speedy
- Reliable
- Able to work if I need to
- Convenient

Complex and important decisions may require many criteria; straightforward decisions may call for only two or three. There is no point in generating long lists for their own sake, and we may decide that some of the least important criteria are not worth bothering with.

Edit the list of criteria produced

When we have listed all the criteria we can think of, we must examine the list carefully, challenging both each objective and the list as a whole:

- Is each criterion necessary?
- Does each say what we really want?
- Is the wording of each clear and unambiguous?
- Are all criteria measurable, or at least clearly checkable? Are dates and times, money, responsibilities, places etc. all defined as necessary?
- Is there duplication or overlap between criteria?
- Does the list concentrate unduly on any aspects?
- Are there any gaps in the list?
- Have we described features when desired outcomes would be more helpful?

After editing, our list of criteria for the journey may look like this:

- Maximum safety
- A relaxed journey
- Within allowable expenses
- Unlikely to suffer delays
- Able to work if I need to
- Shortest door-to-door time

Weight the criteria

Our reaction at this stage may be that no method of travel can meet all our criteria fully. This is true, and we must therefore consider the relative importance (sometimes called the 'utility') we place on each criteria. This will help us, at a later stage, to compare the options available to see which fits our criteria best.

This process may prove difficult to do accurately, as it may require comparison between aspects which are unquantifiable and even difficult to define. It is often subjective, and we shall need to involve as many as possible of those who are affected.

The result of our comparisons is best indicated by weighting each criterion. This is done by giving each a number whose value indicates its importance to us when compared with the others. The larger the number, the more important the criterion to us.

To do this, we must begin by setting a benchmark against which we can compare. It is best to begin at the top, by setting the benchmark against that criterion which is most important to us; to this, we will allocate the highest weight. A weight of 10 is suitable unless we have many criteria between which we can make fine distinctions, when we might prefer a top weight of 50 or even 100.

In our example, we decide that the most important criterion is that of 'maximum safety' and allocate this the 10 weight.

We must next allocate weights to each other criterion. It is best to consider next which criterion is least important to us. We will assume that this is: 'able to work if I need to'.

We must now compare this with our top-weighted criterion, and allocate a weight that shows its relative importance to us. This weight does **not** have to be 1. If we believe all criteria are equally important, they would all receive the weight of 10. In this case, we decide that it is fairly unimportant, and give it the weight 4.

We are now in a position to allocate weights between 10 and 4 to each of the other criteria.

If necessary, we may improve the accuracy of our weighting by carrying out a forced choice comparison of all criteria. This involves comparing each criterion with each other in turn, asking the question 'Which is more important to me in making this decision?' The more important criterion in each comparison will be scored 1; the less important 0. If we cannot distinguish, then each will be scored 0.5. The scores are then added for each criterion:

Maximum safety	A relaxed journey	Within allowable expenses	Unlikely to suffer delays	Able to work if I need to	Shortest door-to-door time
I					
I	0				
I	I	I			
I	I	I	I		
I	0	I	0	0	
5	2	3	I	0	3

Occasionally, it may be possible to improve the accuracy of our weighting by putting money values or some other consistent measure to our criteria. Such an exercise can provide a useful discipline and a few healthy shocks by highlighting the risks attached to some aspects of our decision.

Based on the forced choice comparison, the final list of criteria will now be:

• Maximum safety	10
• Within allowable expenses	8
• Shortest door-to-door time	6
• A relaxed journey	4
• Unlikely to suffer delays	2
• Able to work if I need to	1

Producing such a list will have given us considerable insight into the decision, and make the subsequent stages easier and more successful. We shall be able to communicate with the others involved more effectively, and put them in a better position to give us feedback and help with any necessary changes.

Summary

- It is essential to clarify the criteria of a decision before looking at options or choosing aids
- Criteria are the means of deciding between options and may cover resources, features or outcomes associated with the decision
- It is best to write criteria down, brainstorming first, and then editing the list
- The edited list of criteria should be weighted to indicate their relative importance

Finding options

An option is an alternative or choice available to us when making a decision. One of four approaches may be needed at this stage, depending on the number of options we are aware of:

> *Step 3 – Options*
> - Find options
> - Create options
> - Accept that insufficient options exist
> - Limit the options we need to consider

Find options

We can often use some systematic source of information or method of search. Sources include:

- Colleagues' and friends' knowledge
- Suppliers' catalogues and representatives
- Trade publications
- Newspaper advertisements
- Directories and other reference books
- Electronic databases
- Agents

Create options

Systematic search may not be appropriate or sufficient; we may have to break new ground. The need may be to undertake research, or to conceive new approaches. Thus, if we are: 'Choosing a suitable material for the rotor of our new pump', we may have to undertake some fundamental research to come up with possible options.

Our need may be creative thinking. If we are: 'Looking for a new corporate logo', we will need to undertake a process of brainstorming or other methods of creative thought.

Brainstorming
We discussed 'brainstorming' when talking about criteria (p. 37). The keys to such an approach are:

- Involving other people
- Working against the clock
- Aiming for quantity rather than quality
- Avoiding criticism until we have run dry of ideas

Other ways of generating new ideas include:

- Taking a very similar situation and looking for parallels
- Taking a totally different situation and looking for parallels
- Considering an apparently outrageous idea and asking how it could be made to work
- Listing the characteristics of the ideal solution, asking where or how each could be found, and how they might be combined
- Combining two or more less than ideal possibilities

Accept that insufficient options exist

We may be unable to find any options; going back to our decision of Monday (p.26), we may find that there is no suitable office accommodation in Malvern with 1 000 square feet of floor space. In this situation, we must first review our objectives. If we conclude that 1 000 square feet remains essential, then we will need to move back to the decision definition; maybe we could consider offices elsewhere than in Malvern, or maybe we could manage in some way without additional premises.

If we can find only one option, the decision will be whether to accept or reject it; a binary decision as we described it on Monday (p.30).

Limit options

If we are faced with too many options, our approach at this stage will need to be completely different.

'Sieving' options
The ideal solution is, of course, to consider each option systematically, either accepting it for further, detailed consideration, or rejecting it. To do this requires some instrument – a gauge, sieve or profile – against which this sifting can be carried out swiftly and efficiently. But this can be difficult to do honestly and rationally; there is a temptation to invent arbitrary criteria, act by gut feeling or even at random.

This is the classic situation of recruiters, who, faced with perhaps 500 applications for one vacancy, will carry out a multi-stage process. The first sift is often swift and may be based on little more than the immediate impression of an application. Long-listing may be done on one or two criteria, such as age or qualification level, which may be argued to have little validity – even to be positively damaging – but form an easy means of reducing the options.

When purely personal decisions are being made – choice of house, holiday location, partner or whatever – the reduction of options by quick and arbitrary criteria may be felt acceptable. If we wish to reject properties in Surrey, or the USA, without further thought, we will certainly have fewer options. But even in this kind of decision, we risk eliminating the ideal choice.

When attempting to be rational, three methods are available: random elimination, pre-selection profiling (PSP), and the iterative method.

Random elimination
Random elimination is appropriate when we can find no meaningful way of distinguishing between a large number of options. This would be true, for example, of a competition in which large numbers of entrants answered all questions correctly. In such a situation, random methods such as drawing from a sack or by order of receipt are appropriate.

Pre-selection profiling (PSP)
PSP offers a way forward if it is possible to set meaningful levels to a number of quantitative criteria.

PSP criteria must be both *measurable, valid* and *based on available information.*

Thus a criterion for a car, 'Must be less than 5000mm in length' (the inside length of our garage) is measurable and could be valid, but 'good road-holding' describes a relative and unmeasured criterion (how good is 'good'?).

In the choice of a house, we may set criteria of at least four bedrooms, a double garage and freehold tenure. Such a profile would be simple to work with, and would enable us to reduce the number of options substantially. On the other hand, whilst a minimum lounge length of 7.5m is measurable, it would not be valid if we would be prepared to look at one of 7m; to impose such an arbitrary criterion may eliminate viable options.

PSP criteria cannot be based on prediction. In selecting a book on decision-making from the library shelves, 'must be interesting and helpful', cannot be used for PSP; we could not know until we had read (or tried to read) it.

We will examine the **iterative** method tomorrow.

Infinite options
With decisions involving quantities, there may, at least theoretically, be an infinity of options. Thus there is an infinity of mixes of products we could aim to sell in the next financial year. In such situations, we shall need to set a sensible number of arbitrary stages to reduce the range of options to a workable number:

Option 1: 20% product A, 30% product B, 50% product C
Option 2: 30% product A, 50% product B, 20% product C
Option 3: 40% product A, 50% product B, 10% product C

As the decision-making proceeds and we learn more about the most likely areas of choice, we can refine the possibilities:

Option 2a: 35% product A, 45% product B, 20% product C
Option 2b: 35% product A, 40% product B, 25% product C

The feedback from options to criteria

Whatever method is used to generate options for a decision, thinking about them is almost certain to help us revise our list of criteria. We will discover features or aspects that we had not previously considered, and learn more about the relative importance of the criteria we already have.

Summary

- If our need is to discover existing options, there are numerous sources available
- If no options appear to exist, we may need to undertake creative thinking, or we may need to revise our criteria or decision definition
- If too many options exist, we will need to limit them by random elimination, pre-selection profiling, or use an iterative approach to the decision
- If there is an infinite number of quantitative options, we should set up a series of suitable arbitrary steps, refining them as we gain knowledge
- We should feed back knowledge gained in examining options into our list of criteria

Choosing decision-making aids

Today, we will look at the next step in the decision-making
process, choosing decision-making methods. We will
consider:

Step 4 – Decision-making aids

- The function of decision-making aids
- Arbitrary methods
- Taking advice
- Heuristics
- Elimination
- Graphical and tabular aids
- Statistical aids

We will look at the important subject of group decision-
making methods tomorrow.

The function of decision-making aids

We have come a long way already this week. We know
what decision we are making, why we are making it, what
our aims and criteria are, and what options are open to us.
Sometimes by this stage our thinking has become so clear
that the decision is self-evident. On the other hand, there
may be much work still to do. There are numerous decision-
making aids available to help in the tasks that lie ahead.

The bad news, is that none of these aids actually *make*
decisions. As we noted on Sunday, decisions cannot be
made mechanically; machines cannot commit people to a
course of behaviour. If they could, life would be a lot
simpler and less interesting, and this book would be a waste
of time. At the end of the day, the responsibility for making
and committing to a choice lies with the decision-maker.

A well-chosen decision-making aid can, nevertheless, be of
great value, and in complex decisions may be essential. It
can:

- Provide a framework for logical thinking
- Indicate the information we need
- Help to eliminate the non-essential
- Offer choices in a format which makes comparison
  easier

Not all these functions will be necessary in every decision.

Information
Rational decision-making, by any method, requires
information. We cannot evaluate an option without

knowing a good deal about it. However, there are several important difficulties.

Information usually requires **resources** to obtain. The most obvious resource is time; full information may require more time than we have available. If the decision is needed by next Friday, we will not have time for full market research; if it is needed before the fire gets out of control, we cannot investigate every possible escape route.

Information may also cost money: purchase of books or directories, access to databases, the use of search agents, the costs of travel; we may even need to undertake surveys, research or trials.

Information is often unreliable, especially if gathered hastily. Many decisions are made badly because they are based on poor intelligence – bad observation or perhaps a single piece of anecdotal evidence. Effective decision-makers must always evaluate and be prepared to challenge evidence.

It is possible to have too much information. The art of effective decision-making is to have the relevant information and to eliminate the irrelevant without waste of time. Unfortunately, the coming of computers and IT has made the danger of information surfeit ever more likely. An effective choice of aid will help to focus on the information actually needed.

Choosing appropriate aids
There is a wide range of aids, and it is important to pick the most relevant. A correct choice of aid will depend on factors such as:

- The urgency of the decision (U)
- Its importance (I)
- Its complexity (C)
- The number of options (O)
- Whether it is repeated or one-off (R)

In complex and important decisions, it is often useful to combine a number of aids.

We will now look at each of the main types of aid, and suggest when and how it may be helpful. We will suggest the general suitability of each method according to whether each of the above criteria are high (H), medium (M), or low (L).

Arbitrary aids

Such age-old aids to decision-making as coin-tossing and drawing straws are valid when we cannot distinguish between the options available. They also have the important advantage of giving an appearance of fairness between individuals involved. This makes them ideal in choosing someone to carry out a tricky or unpopular action.

Arbitrary aids may be helpful when: $U = H/M$, $I = M/L$, $C = H/L$, $O = M/L$, $R = L$.

Taking advice

The urge to consult others when making a difficult decision is natural. It offers the possibility of benefiting from their knowledge and experience, of obtaining moral support, and of helping our own thought processes by the act of talking things through with someone else. Sometimes, though, seeking advice may really be an attempt to duck out of responsibility for what should be our decision along.

Seeking advice from others also has dangers. It is never possible to rely on total confidentiality. The chosen individual may have some interest of their own in the subject. We may become involved in a political situation, there may be tensions between the various people we consult, and we may find a need to take sides. We may feel an obligation to accept advice.

If we do seek advice, we may go to those who are experts in the relevant area, those who we believe are friendly and well disposed to, or those who seem to have magical powers.

Consulting experts
It seems natural, when making decisions, to seek and rely on the opinions of others who have expertise in the area. Thus

newly-appointed managers will seek advice on how to act in a tricky situation from their more experienced colleagues; investors may look for a financial advisor to help them decide what shares to buy; proprietors of business will expect their accountants to advise on how to minimise their tax liability.

However, there are also some subjects on which, by their very nature, advice is less valuable than others. Thus advice on employment legislation can be clear and objective. On the other hand, advice on financial investment must always be subjective; if advisors knew when stocks would be going up, they would have retired in luxury years ago. We must always remember that the decision remains ours.

We should never allow ourselves to be overawed by experts. We must ensure we understand what we are told and the reasoning behind it, and be prepared to challenge any aspect about which we have doubts. The more competent the expert, the more ready and able they will be to answer us. We should also be prepared to seek further opinions if we judge them to be necessary.

An occasionally used method of refining expert advise is known as the **Delphi Method.** A question or decision posed, in writing, to each member of a panel of experts. The panel does not meet, but its individual responses are made in writing and then recirculated to the members. From this, members' revised views are obtained, and circulated again. This may be done several times. The aim is that the process will produce a high degree of expert consensus. The method is more appropriate to academic than management use.

Taking expert advise may be helpful when: $U = H/L$, $I = H/M$, $C = H/M$, $O = H/L$, $R = L$.

Consulting friends and family
Most people, when faced with stressful decisions, will look for a partner, close friend, professional counsellor or perhaps a priest with whom to discuss it.

Often the very act of putting the situation into words can do much both to release the tension and to clear our thinking, whether the advice of the other party is helpful or not. As always, we must retain full responsibility for our decision, in their interest and ours.

Consulting friends and family may be helpful when: $U = H/L$, $I = H/L$, $C = M/L$, $O = M/L$, $R = L$.

Consulting oracles and fortune tellers
Resorting to some form of 'magic', whether performed by drug-crazed women in underground caves, as at Delphi, by dissecting animals or observing the flight of birds, as in Rome, or by the present vogue for astrology, has been used by many decision-makers over the ages. This book does not recommend its use. However, some who have resorted to it

in stressful decision-making have found that it helps. It may reveal unconscious attitudes, and can strengthen commitment to a particular course of action – whether this is what the oracle appears to recommend or not.

Heuristics

If we had to make every decision from scratch, life would be impossible. Rules of thumb (technically known as heuristics) are essential in everyday decision-making.

Heuristics are, in effect, ready-made decisions waiting for use. They are short cuts, and enable us to make decisions quickly and with only limited information. We use many unconsciously, and they can be difficult to put into words or figures. It is in this way that craftsmen, experienced business people, managers and professionals make many of their decisions. 'If I skim off another thou, the material will fail.' 'If I raise the price by another pound, this customer will buy from my competitor.' 'The market looks fragile, I will not buy today.'

We may apply some heuristics consciously: 'If the sunset is red, I will not carry my umbrella tomorrow.' 'If their handshake is flabby, I will not employ them.' 'If his eyes are too close together, I cannot trust him.'

Heuristics are essential to life. Indeed, the use of effective heuristics is a key distinction between the successful and the less successful in every field. But they have limitations and dangers.

Quite small differences may make rule of thumb unsuitable. This is especially true of interpersonal situations. Just because reading the riot act to Fred made him pull up his socks does not mean that Tom will react in the same way; he may hit us, or hand in his resignation on the spot. Just as cause-jumping is dangerous when solving problems, so using heuristics without further thought can lead to bad decisions. History does not really repeat itself, and there can be no substitute for accurate data and clear analysis.

Heuristics may be based on poor evidence. Selectors who believe they can judge candidates by the strength of their handshake or the closeness of eyes would do well to review the evidence on which they base their belief. Not only old wives, but many apparently rational individuals are liable to base their beliefs on unchallenged tales.

At their worst, heuristics may be nothing more than a basis for bias and discrimination. How many recruiters, for example, could justify their demand for candidates 'under the age of 35', or their unspoken beliefs about colour, sex or race?

Because so many are subconscious, improving the effectiveness of our heuristics is not easy. We should always strive to be conscious of those we are using, prepared to challenge their effectiveness, and to abandon them when need arises.

Expert systems have been developed in some areas as a computer-based decision-making aid. They may be thought of as computerised heuristics, using the highest expertise available. Expert systems are constructed by feeding into a suitable model the answers given by experts in defined situations. Thus an expert system may be used to help doctors in diagnosis. The construction of the system may be thought of, in highly simplified terms, as presenting a range of symptoms (e.g. blood pressure, temperature, areas of pain etc.) to experienced practitioners, and feeding in their diagnosis. From the results, a most likely diagnosis for combinations of symptoms can then be made available to the user.

Heuristics may be helpful when: $U = H/M$, $I = M/L$, $C = H/L$, $O = H/L$, $R = H/M$.

Elimination (iterative decision-making)

This method depends on a step-by-step approach, and is sometimes called 'iterative decision-making'. It aims to make an effective decision without requiring disproportionate resources of time or effort. We mentioned it yesterday as one method of making decisions in which a very large number of options are available which are difficult to sift. Many people use the method unconsciously in much of their decision-making.

Iterative decision-making begins by taking an option at random. This option is compared with our aim and criteria until either **a**) it becomes clear that it does not match well or **b**) we cannot readily obtain sufficient data to evaluate it. If we reach either of these situations, the option is rejected. If not, it is accepted.

Let us assume that my decision definition is: 'To choose a textbook on elementary statistics'. My criteria are:

> 10 Written in a way I can understand
> 10 Covers the syllabus of my examination
> 8 With test papers and answers for each subject
> 5 Plenty of examples

I am faced with a library shelf of dozens of books. To compare all systematically would be quite impracticable; iterative decision-making is the best approach. In opening the first book I pick off the shelves, I realise immediately that the language is incomprehensible; I put it back. The second book is clear and simple. The contents page shows that it covers the syllabus fully. However, it has no test papers, and I spot few examples; back it goes. The third book seems clear. It covers the syllabus. There are tests at the end of each chapter with answers at the back. It is not so easy to judge the examples, but this is the least important objective. I choose this book, and leave the other three dozen with the reasonable belief that I have made a wise choice without wasting time.

Iterative decision-making may be helpful when: U = H/M, I = M/L, C = M/L, O = H/M, R = H/L.

Graphical and tabular aids

Many people find pictures more helpful than words or figures in evaluating a situation. Most of the statistical aids discussed in the next section can be represented graphically. There are also several well-known and helpful aids to decision-making that use physical layout to clarify their logic and facilitate their use.

The two most common and useful of these are multiple-choice matrices and decision trees. We will now look at each.

Multiple-choice matrices
Decisions in which we have both a number of criteria and a number of options can be depicted as a matrix in which each option is compared against each criterion. Decisions of this type are common in management: which of a number of candidates for a vacancy to appoint; which of a number of makes of equipment or machinery to buy; which of the available sites to choose for the new office, warehouse, factory or shop.

Let us assume that we are filling a vacancy for a manager in our organisation. Our decision definition is: 'Selecting the most suitable candidate to appoint as Customer Services Manager'. We have produced a weighted list of the following criteria:

10	Experienced in customer service work
10	Experience in the widget-selling industry
9	Tactful and diplomatic
8	Supervisory experience
6	Potential for promotion to senior management

We have four candidates for interview, A, B, C and D. We can set up the matrix as follows:

Criteria	Wt	Candidate A	Candidate B	Candidate C	Candidate D
Experienced in customer service work	10				
Experience in the widget-selling industry	10				
Tactful and diplomatic	9				
Supervisory experience	8				
Potential for promotion	6				
Totals					

Having done this, we may find that we already have some of the information we need, from the CVs and application letters the candidates have sent. The matrix will be of great value during the interview process, as it will be used to indicate the need for additional information.

After interview, with the full information available, we are in a position to compare each candidate against each criterion in turn. To the one (or more than one if we cannot distinguish) who meets that objective best, we will allocate the top score (10 is suitable). We will then score the others relative to this. We are *not* scoring on an absolute scale (i.e. 10 = the best possible), but on a relative scale (i.e. 10 = the best option available). It is *not* necessary to score any candidate 1; indeed, if we cannot distinguish against a particular criterion, all should be scored 10.

When we have worked through all criteria in this way, we can multiply the scores by the weights throughout the matrix, and total the results for each candidate:

Criteria	Wt	Candidate A		Candidate B		Candidate C		Candidate D	
			W × Sc		W × Sc		W × Sc		W × Sc
Experienced in customer service work	10	5 Years	100	A little	20	3½ years	70	None	0
		Sc:10		Sc: 2		Sc:7		Sc:0	
Experience in the widget-selling industry	10	2 years	20	10 years	100	2 years	20	1 year	10
		Sc:2		Sc:10		Sc:2		Sc:1	
Tactful and diplomatic	9	Excellent	90	Rather unsure & too direct	18	No problems	72	Average to poor	36
		Sc:10		Sc:2		Sc:8		Sc:4	
Supervisory experience	8	Foreman for 2 years	72	Section Leader 1 year	40	Chargehand for 5 years	80	None	0
		Sc:9		Sc:5		Sc:10		Sc:0	
Potential for promotion	6	Possible	30	Very bright, could go far	60	Uncertain but probably not	6	Already seems overpromoted	0
		Sc:5		Sc:10		Sc:1		Sc:0	
Totals			312		238		248		46

The totals will give a prima facie indication as to how we should make the decision. However, we must interpret them carefully. Thus in the example given, we can say confidently that A is the best choice, and D not worth further consideration. However, it would not be sensible, if A rejects our offer, to assume that C is necessarily the best second choice. The totals are too close, and could be reversed by a few points difference in what are highly subjective scores. We would need to re-examine all scores for B and C, and look carefully at the data (i.e. the interview notes) on which they were based. If we remain uncertain, we may decide to call each in for a further interview to obtain better data.

Before making an offer, we should also complete a review in the way we shall discuss on Saturday.

The value of the multiple-choice matrix lies less in the arithmetic than in the discipline of a framework which requires good evidence and clear focused thinking. It is particularly valuable in group decision-making.

Multiple-choice matrices may be helpful when: U = M/L, I = H/M, C = H/M, O = M/L, R = M/L.

Decision trees

As we saw on Sunday, decisions can frequently be thought of as linked in chains. If we add to the consideration the different choices that can be made at each decision, and the different results these choices might produce, the 'chains' can be thought of as 'trees'.

We may, for example, be deciding whether to undertake design work on a new product. Our initial choice is whether to undertake design work or not. Conventionally, our decision is represented by a square from which the option actions diverge:

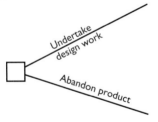

If we do undertake this design, the initial result may or may not be a product that appears worth test marketing. Possible outcomes are conventionally represented by lines diverging from a circle:

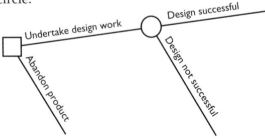

Each of these outcomes would be followed by further decisions, which can be added to the tree:

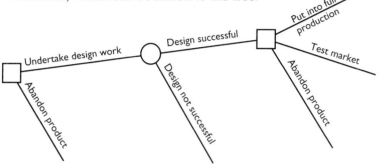

Decision trees can be used to demonstrate the logic of a series of interlinked decisions and the benefits and likelihoods of the various possible outcomes. They can thus be a useful form of analysis at the start of what may prove to be a complex and unfamiliar aid such as new product development.

Decision trees may be helpful when: U = M/L, I = H/M, C = H/M, O = M R = L.

Statistical aids

There is a range of complex and refined statistical aids to various aspects of decision-making. These require an understanding of mathematical theory and an input of resources that make them unsuitable for most personal and management decision-making. There is also a danger that their sophistication may give their results more credibility than is justified.

Statistical decision-analysis is a very extensive field; readers wishing to know more are recommended to look at one of the many text-books on the subject. Today, we will glance quickly at two of the best-known areas; games theory and simulation.

Games theory

Some decisions are competitive; this can be the case in negotiations, commercial competition, international politics or war. In arriving at such decisions, we will need to assess what our competitors are likely to do, and the effects of our own choices on them. Such situations may involve any number of 'players' from two upwards. With three or more players, the possible effects of coalitions must also be considered.

In many cases, the results of the player's or players' action will depend on events over which none have any control, such as the weather. These are often described as 'games against nature'.

If the players are competing for a fixed reward, or payoff, the game is described as a zero-sum game, meaning that whatever one player wins, the other must lose.

Games theory may be helpful when: $U = M/L, I = H/M, C = H/M, O = M/L, R = H/L.$

Models and simulations

Decision-making can be helped by creating a 'model' of the situation, or by simulating it in some way. Most models are in fact mathematical representations of certain aspects of a situation which are designed to behave in the same way as the real thing. In such a decision, for example, as: 'Deciding how many service points should be provided for the station booking office', we may have a criterion: 'No more than one passenger in a hundred should have to wait more than five minutes for service.'

We can devise a set of numbers to represent the arrival of passengers at the booking office, and a further set to represent the length of time it took to deal with each. By combining the two, we can establish the expected range of waiting times with differing numbers of service points open. In doing this we would, of course, be assuming that the numbers we used were representative of the two aspects we were interested in, and our answer would only have a certain probability of meeting our criterion. However, a carefully constructed model of this type would be much more effective than a guess.

Such aids can be invaluable in an appropriate decision-making process. However, mathematical models can only represent a few of the quantifiable aspects of a real-life situation, and it may be necessary to simplify these drastically. In modelling the possible results of the clinical trial of a new drug, for example, we may have to reduce the outcomes to 'successful', 'partly successful' and 'unsuccessful'. In real life, there may be many shades of grey, and unexpected hitches or spin-offs may become crucial.

A valuable form of model is the computer-based spreadsheet. By creating a spreadsheet covering the options available in a decision, it is possible to demonstrate immediately the effect of various possibilities. This 'what if' facility can demonstrate, at the touch of a button, effects that might be difficult to distinguish in other ways. This approach can readily be adapted to the multiple-choice matrix we discussed earlier.

Physical models can be of great help in some kinds of decision, such as the placing of furniture and equipment in a new building.

Modelling may be helpful when: $U = M/L$, $I = H/M$, $C = H$, $O = H/M$, $R = H/L$.

Summary

- Many decision-making aids are available, although none actually make decisions
- The choice of aid depends on the urgency, importance, complexity, number of options and whether the decision is to be repeated
- Relevant information is essential for effective decisions, but obtaining it may require resources
- We should be prepared to challenge the information presented to us
- Decision-making aids include arbitrary aids, taking advice, heuristics, elimination, graphical, tabular and statistical aids

Group decision-making

Many decisions are made by groups rather than individuals.
We will look at this important area under the following
headings:

- The advantages and difficulties of group decision-
  making
- Debating
- Discussing
- Negotiations and bargaining
- Management decision-making

The advantange and difficulties of group decision-making

Groups should be able to offer many powerful advantages
in decision-making. These may include:

- Greater experience and knowledge can be brought to bear than by one individual
- The process of discussion can generate fresh approaches
- The group and its members will feel committed to its conclusions
- Differences can be resolved before they become too damaging

Unfortunately, rational decision-making by groups also presents major difficulties. All the difficulties we will look at on Saturday can be found in group decision-making, together with:

- Interpersonal tensions resulting from the relationships within the group
- Political pressures, hidden agendas and vested interests
- The pulling of rank and status
- The effect of varying individual meeting skills
- Deliberate manipulation

Theoretically, groups could follow any rational process, including all those we looked at yesterday, to great advantage. In practice, groups and the individuals in them are often more concerned with political and personal agendas than with a rational approach to decision-making. Many would actively resist what they would see as an attempt to restrict their freedom of expression.

Faced with a group (or with individual members of a group) who approach the task in this way, it is essential to recognise the situation as quickly as possible. Occasionally it may be productive to bring the difficulties out into the open. More frequently, we can only identify the pressures and work round them as best we may.

When groups are genuinely concerned to behave rationally, the processes we discussed yesterday are just as relevant as they are to individuals. Indeed, they can be of particular help by providing a structure and a discipline. Even recording the progress and results of discussion on flipcharts can be of great value in helping control, creating a methodical record that can help communication with others, and providing a reference for the future. The multiple-choice matrix in particular can be ideal for group use.

In practice, group decision-making is conducted by debate, discussion or, negotiation or bargaining, depending on its purpose and the structure of the group. We will look at each of these, and also the additional factors affecting group decision-making within management.

Debating

Decision-making by more formal groups takes the form of debate. The process of debate varies, depending on the degree of formality of the group, the authority and approach of the Chair, and the approach of group members.

In formal procedure, the intended decision is written down and made known in advance, in the form of a 'motion'. Thus, a motion for a board meeting might be: 'This Board approves the appointment of Bloggs as decision-making consultant to the Board for a term of 12 months at a fee of £5 000.'

At the meeting, the motion would be 'moved' i.e. proposed for acceptance. Members would have the opportunity to speak in favour or against it. It is normally possible for a member to put forward an 'amendment', i.e. a change of wording or an addition to those of the motion. For example, someone may move the amendment: '. . . for a term of six months at a fee of £4 000, subject to renewal with the agreement of this Board'.

Amendments would be voted on first, and then the motion, in its final (or as it is known its 'substantive') form.

The procedures to be followed should be laid down in Rule Books or Standing Orders that are available to all who may have a legitimate interest. These will cover such matters as the notice needed for a motion, who may propose one, whether a seconder is needed, how often a member may speak, how procedural points may be raised, etc.

There can be advantages in formal methods of decision-making in organisations such as public companies, local and national government, large clubs, societies and institutions. In these it is particularly important to ensure that decision-making is seen as thorough, accountable and fair.

To get the best out of this approach, it is essential that we are familiar with the procedures, and know how to use them properly. Those needing to learn more about formal procedure should read one of the many excellent books available which cover the subject.

Discussing

Decision-making by informal groups is probably the commonest method of all. Their approach tends to be loosely structured discussion rather than debate.

Unlike formal groups, informal groups will normally approach a subject area without a form of words or potential decision in front of them. Thus the agenda (if there is one) may include an item: 'Appointment of decision-making consultant'.

During the discussion it is likely that many possible decisions will be aired and fought over, such as whether a consultant is needed at all, what their duties and title should be, for how long, who, and at what fee – even who has the authority to appoint. The effectiveness of such a process varies widely. All-too-often it is time consuming and inefficient. Effectiveness calls for good meeting skills by the Chair, Secretary (if there is one) and every participant.

Here are some suggestions for effectiveness in leading informal groups:

- Appoint a leader and scribe or secretary
- Use visible working: flipchart or board
- Clarify the decision to be made, write it down and keep it visible from the start
- Agree the process to be used, and ensure it is understood and followed with discipline
- Restrain the verbose and encourage the shy
- Distinguish facts from opinions
- Separate creative thinking and criticism
- Judge the moment to press for a decision with care; not too soon, not too late
- Record decisions at the meeting and get commitment
- Thank everyone
- Act

Here are some suggestions for successful participation in both formal and informal group decision-making:

- Prepare your case, including facts and arguments, well in advance
- Assess who is likely to be a supporter and an opponent, and why
- Prepare the ground by individual 'pre-meetings' or lobbying, if this seems likely to be helpful
- Listen and watch carefully, to assess others' agendas; be ready to form helpful alliances
- Time the contribution with care; sometimes aiming to pre-empt others may be best; sometimes waiting until others have run out of steam may be best
- Challenge any ambiguities and doubts about what is being decided
- When the time comes, stand up, speak and then shut up
- Remain polite and cool at all times

Negotiation and bargaining

These differ from other forms of group decision-making in that they are carried out in groups with two or more distinct 'sides' or parties with clearly different interests. The number of people on each side can vary. The distinction between the two is fine, but 'bargaining' is more frequently used in the narrow process of agreeing a price for specific goods or services, and 'negotiation' in establishing broader agreement between parties.

There may be elements of negotiation in any form of group decision-making if it becomes clear that two (or more) differing views can only be reconciled by some form of trade-off, or matched concessions. The best outcome will always be a jointly made decision, but we should always be alert to the possibility of adopting a negotiating stance to avoid stalemate.

Successful negotiation
Here are some guidelines for success in negotiation:

- Clarify objectives
- Decide what compromises (if any) are possible
- Adopt a win/win style
- Begin by explaining overall aims and constraints, but *not* specific objectives
- Invite the other party to do the same
- Listen carefully to what they say and what they leave out
- Avoid dogmatic statements
- Get the other party to suggest figures (e.g. price) first
- Do not agree a point too soon. Hold back to trade against concessions from the other party
- Never rub the other party's face in the dirt; offer a face-saving formula

Taken from M. Peel *Introducing Management in a Week* (1995) Hodder & Stoughton.

Management decision-making

Much management decision-making is done by groups,
either formally or informally. All that we have already said
will, therefore, be relevant to managers, but there are also
additional factors.

The way managers make decisions depends on the culture
and style of their organisation. Local and national
government, the armed forces, large public companies,
smaller organisations, family firms and professional
practices are all likely to approach the task in different ways.

There is also an overall culture of management which
changes through time; it would not be possible for any
manager to work now in Britain in the way all management
was carried out 100, or even 50 years ago. Successful
managers must also take account of this; those who do not
would soon have ; 'trouble at t'mill'.

Summary

- Group decision-making offers both powerful
  advantages and serious disadvantages
- Some groups actively resist attempts to rationalise
  their decision-making process
- Formal group decision-making takes place through a
  process of structured debating; we must know and
  use the rules
- Informal groups need skilled leadership
- In both formal and informal groups, participants need
  skills including preparation, assessing others,
  lobbying, listening, timing, effect presentation, and
  coolness

- Group decisions may be made by bargaining or negotiation; each requires specific skills
- Management decision-making methods will depend on the culture of the organisation.

Decision review

Before committing ourselves to a decision, however we have made it, we need to make a final review. Like everything else about the process, how long this review takes, and the methods we use, will depend on the importance and urgency of the decision. It might take seconds, it could take months, but it is always worth doing. We must review our decision from several angles:

Step 6 – Decision review
- Recheck of process and information
- Opportunity costs
- Risk analysis
- Protection
- Escape

Recheck of process and information

Mistakes occur in even the best-regulated establishments,
and before implementing our decision, it is always worth
rechecking our choice and use of process, aids and
information.

As always with checking, it is better done by someone else;
they should be less biased, and they are more likely to spot
mistakes, gaps and illogicalities. Also, many of the most
common and serious sources of error in decision-making are
subjective. A second opinion is more likely to spot where
these have come into play.

These subjective sources of error in decision-making
include:

- Do I really want to be rational?
- Self-image
- Bias and hang ups
- Attitude to risk
- 'Framing'
- 'Non-rational escalation of commitment'

Do I really want to be rational?
Perhaps the worst difficulty of all is to give an honest
answer to the question 'Do I really want to make a rational
decision?' Quite often, we know exactly what we want to
do, but feel an obligation to go through some show of
thinking about it. We may feel twinges of conscience, we
may be looking to have our instinctive choice confirmed, or
we may hope to be able to justify it to other people. But

unless we are honestly prepared to change our instinctive view, time spent on rational analysis will be time wasted.

Self-image

Our own self-image – the sort of person we believe we are or would like to be – is another source of decision-making error.

For some, fearless decisiveness is part of a macho self-image. Others may feel the need for exhaustive examination of every alternative before making the simplest choice. If our decision leads to difficulty or criticism, many of us feel doubt and struggle with our conscience as to the rightness of reviewing or changing it. If, for example, we see ourselves as caring, we will be deeply reluctant to sack an employee or make them redundant. If we see ourselves as ruthless entrepreneurs, we may derive satisfaction from doing so. If our self-image is of thoroughness and attention to detail, we will be attracted to options which offer opportunities to demonstrate this. If we see ourselves as firm and decisive, we may prefer simpler choices.

Attitude to risk

Cowardice, whether physical or moral, is an enemy of effective decision-making. Many decisions – sometimes even those that are seemingly simple and routine – may require courage both to make and to implement.

The effect of such stress varies. Faced with the risks inherent in even a simple decision, some people become indecisive and vacillating; they put off a choice until overtaken by events. Those who get a buzz out of living dangerously will relish the opportunity to demonstrate their decisiveness and reinforce their macho image. Some may try to shift the responsibility to someone else. Others will release the tension by making a snap, panic decision which they may live to regret.

Bias and hang-ups

We all have biases; beliefs that we refuse to challenge under any but the strongest of pressures. These may be moral, religious or political convictions, or simple beliefs we have accepted, often from an unknown source, without question.

Our leisure interests, where we live or used to live, the clubs and societies we belong to and where we were at school or college often affect our feelings. 'Blood is thicker than water', 'The old school tie' and many similar sayings explain a thousand irrationally made decisions.

It is, of course, impossible to rid ourselves of the many biases and preconceptions, dogmas, beliefs, and assumptions we all have. In some decisions, this is the only factor of importance. If we are selecting someone to join our team, the need for them to fit in with us and the existing members – the 'chemistry' as it is often called – must be a highly weighted criterion.

The best way of coping with biases and hang-ups of all kinds is to ensure that we acknowledge their existence at the start of the process. In making important decisions we should write down those that may come into play, and keep the list in front of us, so as to allow for them and keep them in perspective. If we are working with others, it is good practice to clear the air at the start of the process by admitting biases openly. In reviewing the process, we should look carefully for any that have affected the result.

'Framing'

Decisions may be affected by the context in which they are made, and the way either alternatives or options are presented or perceived. It can make a big difference whether we see our plate as half full or half empty; whether we look on a change as primarily an end or a beginning.

The word 'framing' is sometimes used to describe the way a decision is presented, or the way it is perceived. Thus we may see the purchase of new delivery vehicles as a necessity to save on the maintenance costs. We could approach the same decision from the angle of improving the image of the organisation, or of improving drivers' productivity. If we frame a decision negatively, as a damage limitation or an unfortunate necessity, we will approach it differently from a positive framing, i.e. as a key to growth and improvement.

Making more than one decision at the same time can have a big effect by suggesting a linkage between them which does not exist, framing the lesser in the context of the greater (if we're spending £10 000, what does an extra £1 000 matter, we may ask?) or just distracting our attention. If, for example, we are changing offices, we are far more likely to buy new office furniture than if we remained in the old premises. If we are buying a new car, we may well buy expensive accessories that we would not have considered if we had retained the old one. If we buy a new pc, we will be tempted to add a new printer, even though the old one does all we need.

Before making any important decision, we should always identify and challenge the way we have framed it. Behind every crisis lies an opportunity. Review gives us a final chance of reframing.

'Non-rational escalation of commitment'
It is possible to become emotionally involved with the evolving decision itself; what has been called the 'non-rational escalation of commitment' (M Bazerman, (1990)

Judgement in Managerial Decision-Making, John Wiley). This can be seen most clearly in some meetings, when a possible decision is tentatively suggested, discussed, and gradually becomes the focus of strong feelings. What began life as no more than a suggestion ends up as an ideal for and against which individuals feel ready to fight and die.

The same process occurs in the mind of individuals. As the amount of time and effort we have invested in a particular option grows, so we feel increasing attachment to it as our brainchild and creation. It is important to stand back at intervals during consideration of an option and remind ourselves of the existence of others. Review should include checking whether this effect has operated during the process.

Opportunity costs

The opportunity costs of a course of action are the benefits that we could have obtained if we had done something else instead. If that something else is one of the options we have considered in making our decision – buying machine A rather machine B, for example – then we will already have taken it into account. However, the something else may be completely unrelated to the decision; in choosing which machine to buy we may, for example, have been planning to use cash which might otherwise have been available to pay staff Christmas bonuses.

This may have been picked up at the start of the process; we may already have decided that the cash should be spent on a machine rather than staff bonuses. But if the situation is only revealed during the final review, we will need to backtrack – to move back up the decision chain that we looked at on Monday (p.26).

Risk analysis

Decisions, however well made, are liable to go wrong. Because they look to the future, there will always be the need to forecast, with the varying and sometimes high degree of uncertainty this inevitably brings.

Many of the most important decisions of recent years have been marked by appalling errors of forecasting: huge cost and time overruns on major civil engineering works; the human suffering and industrial devastation resulting from erroneous economic policy decisions; the destruction and loss of life from mistaken war strategies; basic marketing blunders; stock markets that have gone down instead of up; failure to predict storms and tempests.

There are two kinds of risk incurred by decision-making; the risk that we may be prevented from implementing our decision, and the risk that, having implemented it, it may not produce the results we expect. Risk assessment therefore involves answering the questions:

- What may go wrong to prevent us behaving as we have decided?
- What may go wrong as a result of behaving as we have decided?

What may go wrong to prevent us behaving as we have decided? With this question, we are exploring the possibility that we may not be able to carry out our decision as we plan to. We must identify obstacles that may force us to turn aside or back.

The chosen behaviour may prove impossible. We may find, for example, that the candidate to whom we have decided to offer employment has already accepted another post, or that the train we had planned to catch has been cancelled.

The circumstances may not prove to be what we expect. The rise in share prices, which we hope will enable us to sell for a quick profit, for example, may not happen: the autumn weather may be the wettest for years, ruining the crop we sowed in the expectation of dry weather.

What may go wrong as a result of behaving as we have decided? We must consider the possibility that we are able to act exactly as we decide, but that the results are not what we expect. Thus the reprimand we give to our subordinate may cause him to hit us rather than mend his ways.

We may, for example, decide to install a system of performance appraisal in our organisation, based on criteria such as:

- To improve morale
- To help managers to manage more effectively
- To develop individual members of staff

The system has been installed exactly as we had planned, but after six months:

- Morale has sunk to rock bottom
- Managers are complaining of overwork
- The training needs identified by the system exceed the available budget by 300%

If we had conducted a systematic risk analysis before acting, these effects might have been foreseen and avoided.

Sometimes, the failure of a decision may have far more impact than success. Thus to obtain an effective replacement for an out-of-date pc in our office may be no more than routine: it might produce a marginal speeding up of work. On the other hand, to choose one that did not do what was needed could bring our operation to a stand still.

Worst of all, there may sometimes be a total lack of match between actual and expected outcome, whether for better or worse. We may be aiming at improved morale, for example, and find that our experience in appraisal systems is so valuable it becomes a marketable product, in the form of a consultancy service. On the other hand, we may find that an unskilled appraisal causes one of our key people to leave, join a competitor, and take with them the bulk of our profitable business. The bigger the decision, the greater the risk of such difficulties. Systematic risk assessment give us the best change of avoiding them.

Probability

We must now ask, of each of the risks we have foreseen, 'What is the probability that this will happen?' The 'probability' of an event is the likelihood that it will occur. The concept is similar to the odds quoted by a bookmaker; what are the chances of my horse winning? Statisticians define a probability of 1.0 as absolute certainty that an event will occur, and 0.0 as absolute certainty it will not happen. Virtually every event, therefore, has a probability somewhere between the two; the probability of a coin landing heads up is (or should be) 0.5. Probability is a major area of statistical theory, and those needing a thorough knowledge should read one of the many appropriate texts covering the subject. However, although statistical analysis of the probability of an event can show us what the odds are, no analysis can show us what will actually happen.

In many cases, it will be adequate to make a quick, subjective assessment of probability. However, as with judging distances, the mind is subject to certain illusions when assessing probability. If we are aware of these, we have a much better chance of avoiding them.

We tend to overestimate the probability of unlikely events, especially when they are supported by anecdotal evidence. Thus we may feel that the likelihood of being mugged whilst walking in London is high, and ascribe a probability of, say, 0.01 (1 chance in 100). In fact, the probability of such an event is nearer to 0.0000001 (1 chance in 10 000 000). The prosperity of the insurance industry depends heavily on this effect.

We tend to underestimate the probability of common events, especially when we hope to avoid them; there is an element of wishful thinking. Thus we may feel that the chances of rain spoiling the outdoor concert we have bought tickets for are not too bad, and ascribe a probability of, say, 0.1 (1 chance in 10) when the actual probability is likely to be nearer to 0.33 (1 chance in 3).

Threat
We will need to assess the degree of threat to which our decision is subject, bearing in mind the seriousness and probability of the risks we have identified. An improbable but serious risk is, of course, a greater threat than a highly probable but trivial risk. Should we find any risks which we judge are both highly serious and highly probable, we will want to give them immediate and urgent thought, possibly to the extent of revising or rescinding our decision. All but the most trivial threats will call for protective action.

Protection

If we do identify serious threats, either to the execution of the decision, or resulting from it once carried out, further systematic thought will be necessary. Our first aim will usually be to prevent the threat operating, but we may also feel the need to set up a contingency plan in case it does. There may also be some threats we have no option but to live with.

Thus in performance appraisal decision we considered earlier, we may decide the following.

Morale sinks to rock bottom
We cannot prevent damage to morale in an exercise of this nature, but we can try to reduce it by careful briefing of all involved, training of all who will conduct appraisals, and continuous monitoring after introduction.

Managers complain of overwork
They always will, so we will live with this one.

Training needs identified by the system exceed the available budget by 300%
This we can prevent by allocating training budgets to all appraisors, together with explanation to them of the many non-course methods of developing staff.

Escape

To change a decision, once made, feels to many people like an act of weakness. Whilst frequent or unjustifiable changes are certainly weak, there can be many situations in which the sensible, strong course is to abandon or change what we have decided. Until the action has been carried out, no decision should be regarded as final.

We should always face the possibility and consequences of needing to change a decision *before* finalising it. Anticipation can do much to reduce the difficulty.

This approach requires four things for success. We need:

- Appropriate methods of monitoring progress
- To avoid inescapable commitment and irrecoverable expense until and unless it becomes inevitable
- A contingency plan, complete with public relations angles, ready for implementation
- The moral courage to do what is necessary at the right moment

Thus we may decide to monitor implementation of the performance appraisal system by ensuring that documentation is completed on time, by speaking weekly to appraisors, and by informal contacts with a sample of appraisees. Should we decide that serious harm is being done, we may be ready to suspend the operation, perhaps with suitable, prepared justification. Excuses are not generally regarded as part of effective management, but it is better to have a good one ready than to be caught without when one is needed.

Summary

- Both process and information should be checked before implementing a decision
- Rational process is pointless if we know what we want
- Insight into our self-image, biases and hang-ups, attitudes towards risk and the 'frame' in which we approach a decision are essential
- 'Non-rational escalation of commitment' to an option should be avoided
- The opportunity costs of a decision may effect its validity
- We should assess the seriousness and probability of threats to a decision
- We should protect the decision against serious threats, and if necessary provide contingency plans
- The possibility of needing to change a decision should be considered before it is made

Further *Successful Business in a Week* **titles from Hodder & Stoughton and the Institute of Management all at £5.99**

0340 59856 5	Finance for Non–Financial Managers in a Week	☐
0340 63152 X	Introducing Management in a Week	☐
0340 62742 5	Introduction to Bookkeeping and Accounting in a Week	☐
0340 63153 8	Managing Information in a Week	☐
0340 62737 9	Succeeding at Interviews in a Week	☐
0340 60896 X	Successful Appraisals in a Week	☐
0340 60893 5	Successful Assertiveness in a Week	☐
0340 57640 5	Successful Budgeting in a Week	☐
0340 59813 1	Successful Business Writing in a Week	☐
0340 59855 7	Successful Career Planning in a Week	☐
0340 62032 3	Successful Computing for Business in a Week	☐
0340 62740 9	Successful Customer Care in a Week	☐
0340 63154 6	Successful Decision-Making in a Week	☐
0340 62741 7	Successful Direct Mail in a Week	☐
0340 64330 7	Successful Empowerment in a Week	☐
0340 59812 3	Successful Interviewing in a Week	☐
0340 60895 1	Successful Leadership in a Week	☐
0340 57466 6	Successful Market Research in a Week	☐
0340 55539 4	Successful Marketing in a Week	☐
0340 60894 3	Successful Meetings in a Week	☐
0340 61137 5	Successful Mentoring in a Week	☐
0340 57522 0	Successful Motivation in a Week	☐
0340 55538 6	Successful Negotiating in a Week	☐
0340 52876 1	Successful Presentation in a Week	☐
0340 56531 4	Successful Project Management in a Week	☐
0340 56479 2	Successful Public Relations in a Week	☐
0340 62738 7	Successful Purchasing in a Week	☐
0340 57523 9	Successful Selling in a Week	☐
0340 57889 0	Successful Stress Management in a Week	☐
0340 58763 6	Successful Time Management in a Week	☐
0340 61889 2	Successful Training in a Week	☐
0340 62103 6	Understanding BPR in a Week	☐
0340 56850 X	Understanding Just in Time in a Week	☐
0340 61888 4	Understanding Quality Management Standards in a Week	☐
0340 58764 4	Understanding Total Quality Management in a Week	☐
0340 62102 8	Understanding VAT in a Week	☐

All Hodder & Stoughton books are available from your local bookshop or can be ordered direct from the publisher. Just tick the titles you want and fill in the form below. Prices and availability subject to change without notice.

To: Hodder & Stoughton Ltd, Cash Sales Department, Bookpoint, 39 Milton Park, Abingdon, Oxon, OX14 4TD. If you have a credit card you may order by telephone - 01235 831700.

Please enclose a cheque or postal order made payable to **Bookpoint Ltd** to the value of the cover price and allow the following for postage and packing:

UK & BFPO: £1.00 for the first book, 50p for the second book and 30p for each additional book ordered up to a maximum charge of £3.00.

OVERSEAS & EIRE: £2.00 for the first book, £1.00 for the second book and 50p for each additional book.

Name. ....

Address ....

....

If you would prefer to pay by credit card, please complete:
Please debit my Visa/Mastercard/Diner's Card/American Express (delete as appropriate) card no:

☐☐☐☐☐☐☐☐☐☐☐☐☐☐☐☐

Signature. .... Expiry Date ....